# Fiddle Time Jo

## Violin accompaniment book

## Kathy and David Blackwell

---

**Teacher's note**

These duet parts are written to accompany the tunes in *Fiddle Time Joggers*. They are an alternative to the piano accompaniments or audio tracks, and are not designed to be used with those items. With the exceptions of Nos. 4, 43, and 46, these parts may be used with violins playing together with violas (using *Viola Time Joggers* and playing the ensemble parts where appropriate); in a few pieces some details are different between the two books, for example some bar numbers and introductions. A separate viola duet book is available providing duet parts for all the additional tunes in *Viola Time Joggers*.

We are grateful to Simon Stace for all his help in road-testing these duets.

Kathy and David Blackwell

---

Great Clarendon Street, Oxford OX2 6DP, England
This collection © Oxford University Press 1998, 2001, 2005, 2013 and 2022
Unless marked otherwise, all pieces (music and words) are by Kathy and David Blackwell and are
© Oxford University Press. All traditional pieces are arranged by Kathy and David Blackwell and are
© Oxford University Press. Unauthorized arrangement or photocopying of this copyright material is ILLEGAL.

Kathy and David Blackwell have asserted their right under the Copyright,
Designs and Patents Act, 1988, to be identified as the Composers of this Work.

ISBN 978-0-19-356200-4

Music and text origination by Katie Johnston
Printed in Great Britain on acid-free paper by
Halstan & Co. Ltd, Amersham, Bucks.

# Contents

# 1. Bow down, O Belinda

# 2. Under arrest!

KB & DB

Say the word 'rest' quietly to yourself as you play.

# 3. Someone plucks, someone bows

Traditional
Words KB & DB

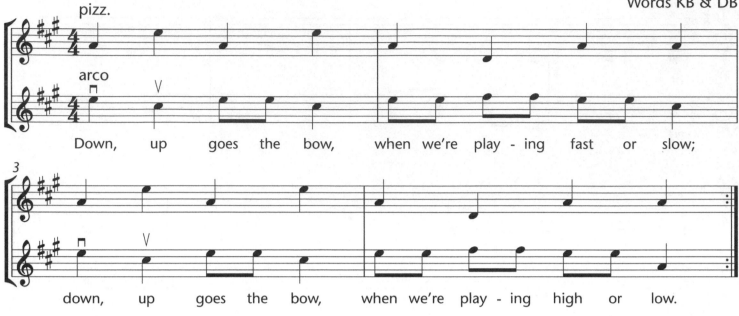

pizz.

arco

Down, up goes the bow, when we're play - ing fast or slow;

down, up goes the bow, when we're play - ing high or low.

# 4. Down up

KB & DB

arco

*f marcato*

Down up E string,

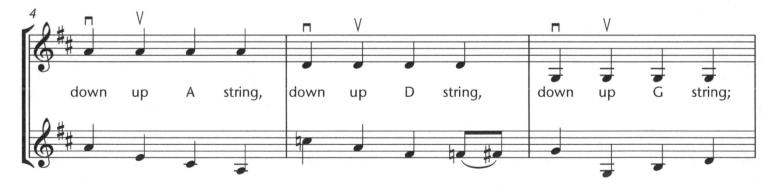

down up A string, down up D string, down up G string;

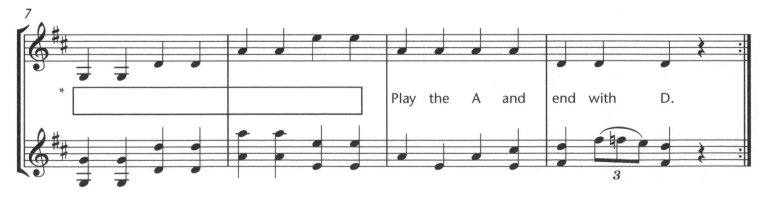

*

Play the A and end with D.

\* Fill in the letter names of these notes.

## 5. Two in a boat

American folk tune

## 6. London Bridge

English folk tune

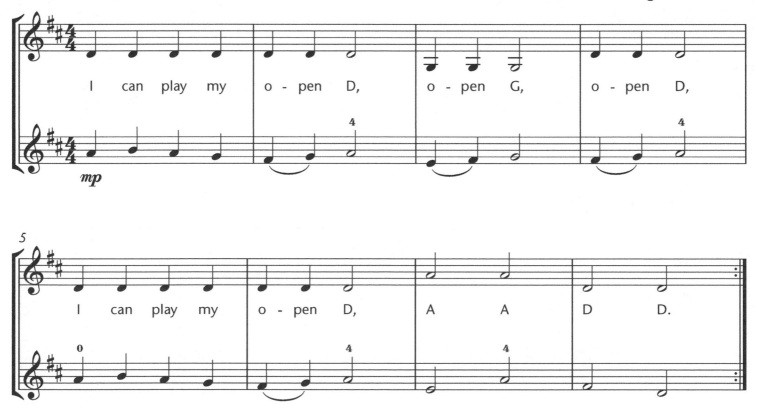

I can play my o - pen D, o - pen G, o - pen D,

I can play my o - pen D, A A D D.

# 7. Fast lane

KB & DB

Try even faster the second time through!

# 8. In flight

KB & DB

**Calmly**

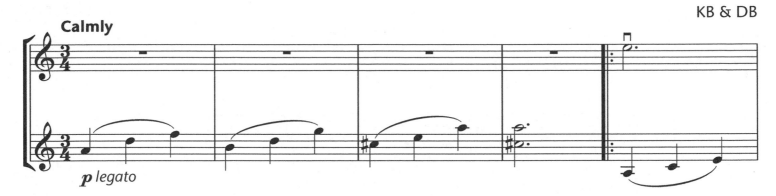

*p legato*

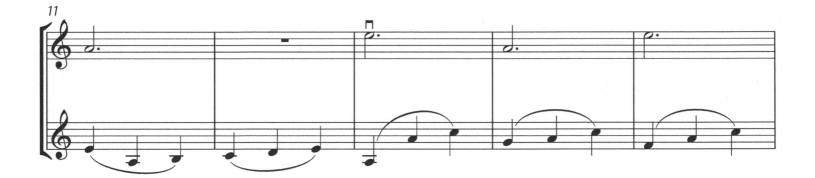

In the rests, let your bow make a circle as you swoop and soar like a bird.

# 9. Lift off!

KB & DB

Lift your bow off in each of the rests and let it orbit! (Make a circle with your right arm.)

# 10. Katie's waltz

KB & DB

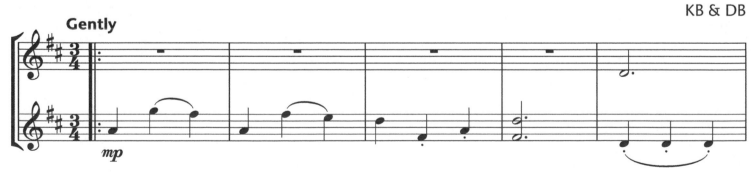

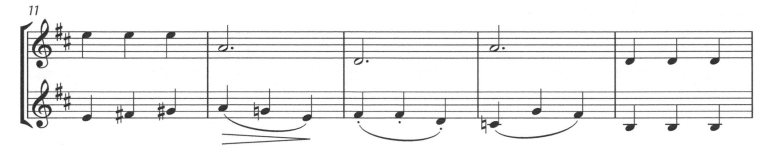

## 11. Copy cat

KB & DB

Can you play what I play? D D E E

Can you play what I play? Play it now with me.

Can you play what I play? A A B B

Can you play what I play? Play it now with me.

## 12. Tap dancer

KB & DB

* Hold the bow upright and tap the screw end of the bow on your music stand.

# 13. Rhythm fever

KB & DB

**Rock tempo**

Rhy - thm fe - ver, 1 2 3 4

feel the beat, 1 2 3 4 feel the rhy - thm, 1 2 3 4

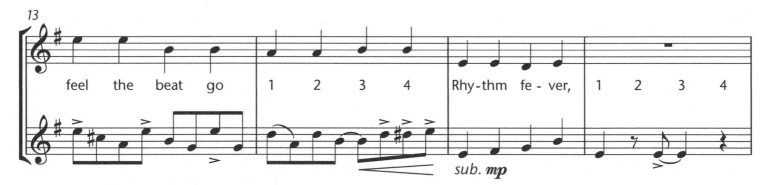

in your feet. 1 2 3 4 Feel the rhy - thm as you play it,

feel the beat go 1 2 3 4 Rhy - thm fe - ver, 1 2 3 4

rhy - thm fe - ver, 1 2 3 4 rhy - thm fe - ver, oh yeah!

## 14. Here it comes!

KB & DB

Through the teeth and | past the gums, so | watch out, tum - my, | here it comes!

Through the teeth and | past the gums, so | watch out, tum - my, | here it comes!

\* Think of a foody rhythm and play it on these notes.

## 15. So there!

KB & DB

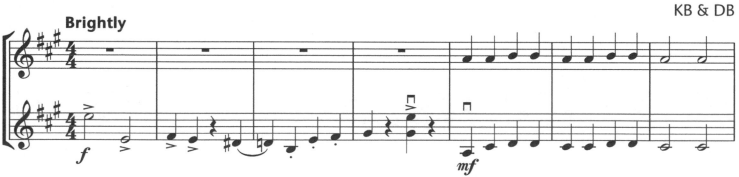

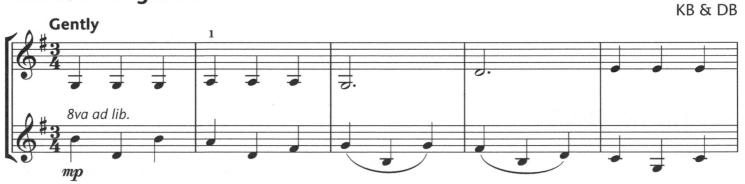

## 16. Rowing boat

KB & DB

## 17. Ally bally

Scottish folk tune

## 18. Tiptoe, boo!

KB & DB

**Spookily!**

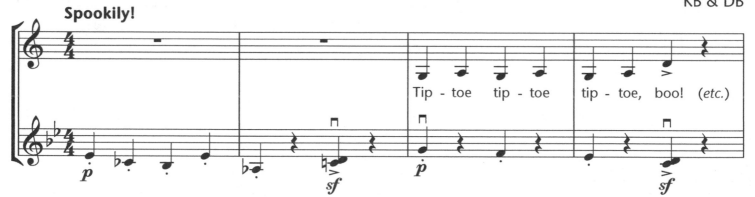

Tip - toe    tip - toe    tip - toe,  boo!  (*etc.*)

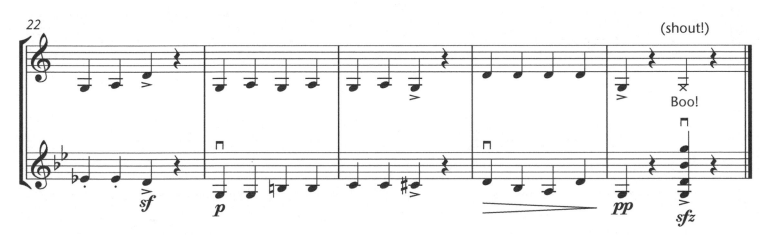

The pupil's part may also be played pizzicato.

## 19. Travellin' slow

KB & DB

## 20. Lazy cowboy

KB & DB

## 21. Off to Paris

French folk tune

## 22. Clare's song

KB & DB

# 23. City lights

KB & DB

**Gutsy**

## 24. The three friends

Finnish folk tune

## 25. Peace garden

KB & DB

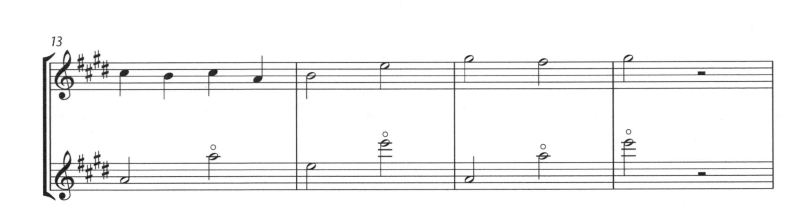

# 26. Summer sun

KB & DB

## 27. Phoebe in her petticoat

American folk tune

Swap parts when you do the repeat.

## 28. Ready, steady, go now!

KB & DB

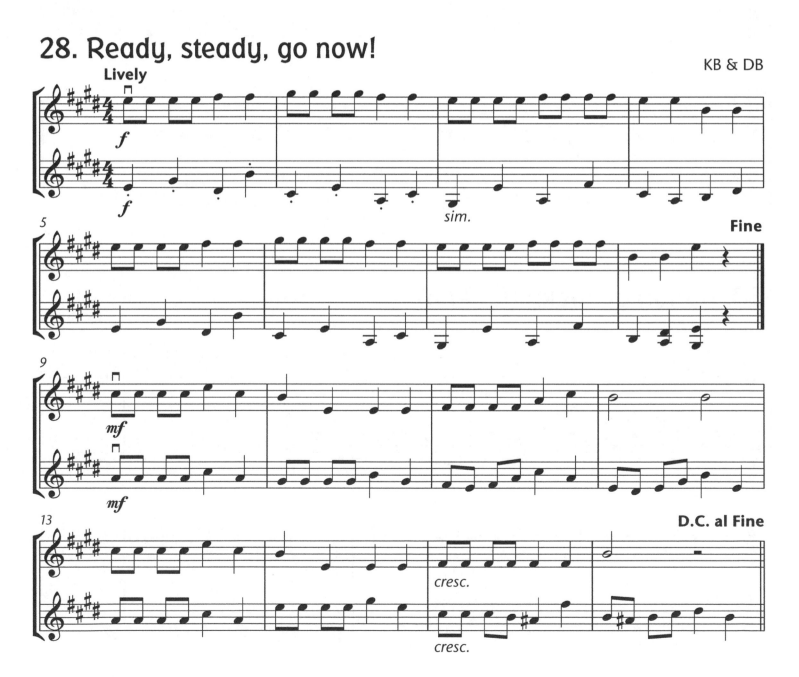

# 29. Cooking in the kitchen

KB & DB

# 30. Happy go lucky (for Iain)

KB & DB

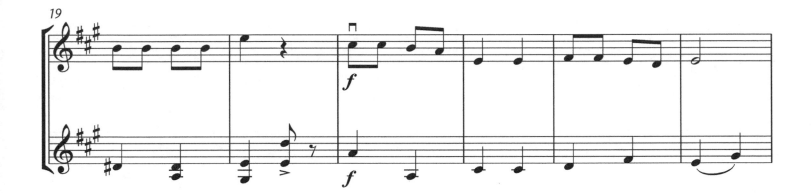

# 31. The mocking bird

Gently like a lullaby

American folk tune

# 32. Algy met a bear

KB & DB
Words anon.

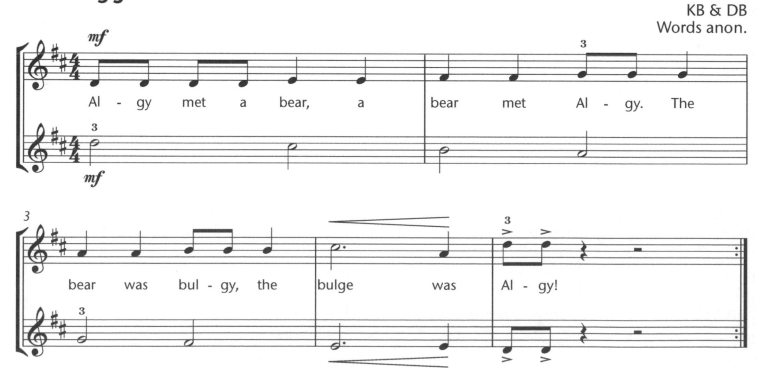

Al - gy met a bear, a bear met Al - gy. The

bear was bul - gy, the bulge was Al - gy!

Swap parts when you do the repeat.

26

# 33. Listen to the rhythm

KB & DB

# 34. Cattle ranch blues

KB & DB

## 35. In the groove

KB & DB

## 36. Stamping dance

Czech folk tune

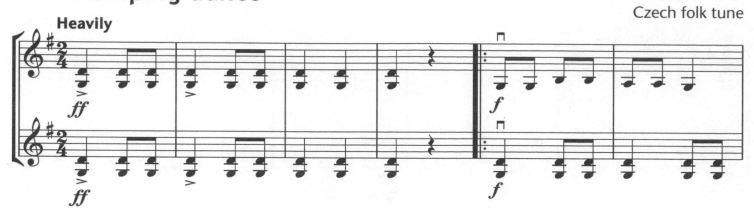

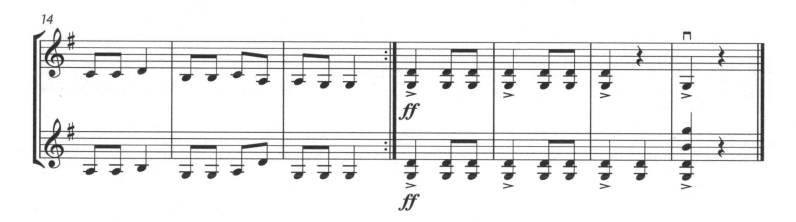

## 37. Distant bells

KB & DB

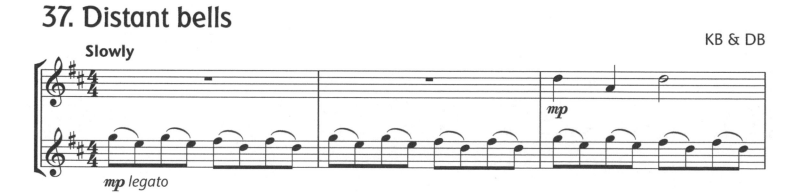

## 38. Lazy scale

KB & DB

# 39. The old castle

**With a singing tone**

KB & DB

**rit.**

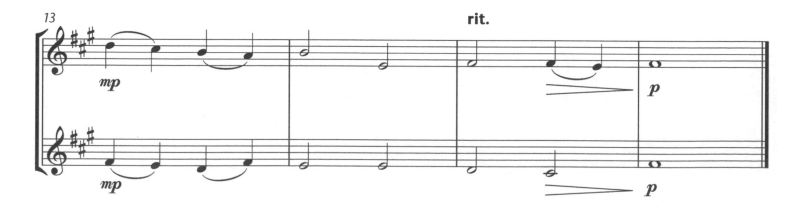

# 40. Rocking horse

KB & DB

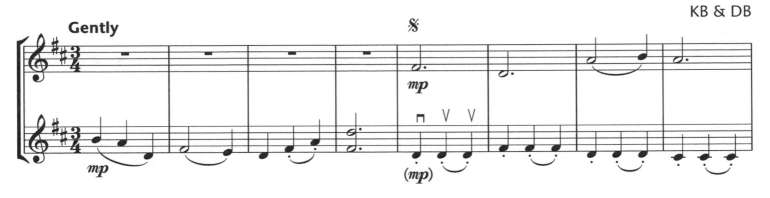

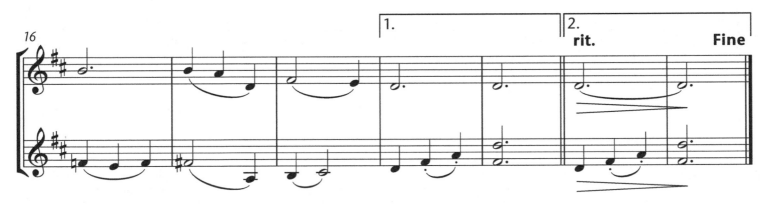

# 41. Patrick's reel

KB & DB

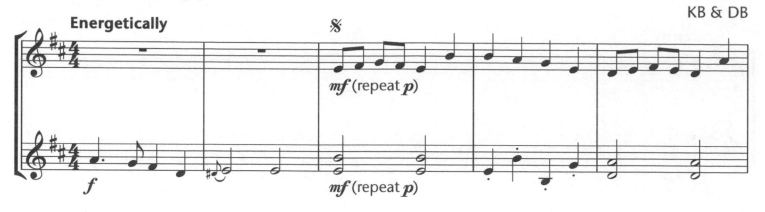

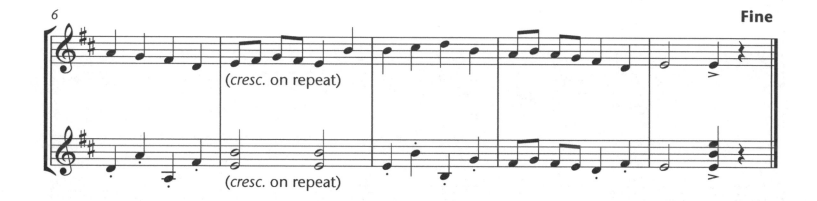

# 42. Calypso time

KB & DB

**Carnival tempo**

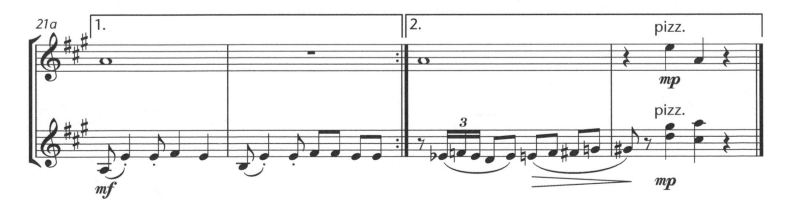

# 43. Knock, knock!

**Jokingly!**

KB & DB

Make up some other 'Knock, knock' jokes and play them on your violin.

# 44. Rocky mountain

American folk tune

**Lively**

## 45. Carrion crow

American folk tune

# 46. Flying high

KB & DB

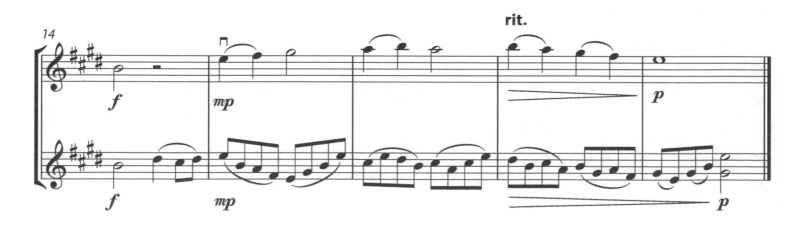

## 47. Fiddle Time

KB & DB